JAIME R. CARLO-CASELLAS, PH.D

Will I be Next?

Gun Violence in America

Mass massacres do not have to be conventional practice in American society.

ISBN: 979-8-89216-030-8 (Paperback)

Library of Congress Control Number: 2024915186

BOOKMARC
A L L I A N C E

BookmarcAlliance
California, USA
www.bookmarcalliance.com

Statement of Originality

I, Jaime R. Carlo-Casellas, certify that this book is based on my study, experience, and research. Recognizing the concern for plagiarism, I have acknowledged in the form of endnotes all material and sources used in its preparation, whether books, articles, reports, lecture notes, or any other kind of document, electronic or personal communication.

Other Books by Jaime R. Carlo-Casellas

Anguish & Joy / Amargura y Deleite: A Journey to Serenity / Una jornada hacia la serenidad

Chaos & Bliss / Caos y Éxtasis: A Journey to Happiness: Poetry and Verse to Enlighten the Mind / Una Jornada a la Felicidad: Poemario para Iluminar la Mente

Mindfulness for the Common Man—to survive trauma, abuse, and recovery

Mindfulness: To Learn That All Lives Can't Matter Until All Lives Matter—That We All Descend from the Same Maternal Womb

Race Does Not Exist—We All Descend From the Same Maternal Lineage (with Philip Drucker, Esq. as coauthor)

Solo Contamos con Una Vida—Cómo Vivirla sin Sufrimiento

Ubuntu: We Are All One, Descendants of Anthropoids— To Build a More Humanitarian Universe (with Philip Drucker, Esq. as coauthor. In press)

Foreword

Mass shootings are a topic we have all been hearing a lot about. It comes up in sessions with my patients, and most recently, it came up at a dinner party where the discussion focused on how immune we have become to the latest shooting we hear in the news. As a psychologist, I understand people are scared, and our feeling of immunity helps us feel safe when the next shooting could involve you or me.

In a world where gun violence has become an all too familiar headline, where tragedies unfold in schools, workplaces, and public spaces, a chilling question lingers in the minds of countless individuals: *Will I Be Next?* It is a question that echoes through our communities, a haunting reminder of the pervasive nature of this devastating epidemic. Gun violence has transcended borders, ideologies, and backgrounds, leaving no one untouched and forcing us all to confront the harsh reality that no one is truly safe.

Dr. Carlo-Casellas's book delves deep into the heart of the issue, seeking to shed light on the multifaceted layers that contribute to the staggering prevalence of gun violence in our society. By examining the intertwined factors of mental health, social inequality, cultural influences, and the political landscape, we hope to uncover the root causes that allow gun violence to persist unchecked.

At its core, *Will I Be Next? Gun Violence in America* strives to catalyze change, challenging the status quo and demanding action. It recognizes this crisis's urgency and our collective responsibility to combat it. Through a thoughtful exploration of the complexities surrounding this issue, Dr. Carlo-Casellas aims to inspire dialogue, empathy, and informed decision-making that can lead to meaningful solutions.

The pages of this book will introduce you to the chilling facts about gun control, mental illness, and devastating death statistics by guns. It explores the disarray of the NRA, the pros and cons of the Second Amendment, and the actions of courts and legislation. By giving voice to these diverse perspectives, Dr. Carlo-Casellas hopes to bridge the gap between statistics and human lives, reminding readers that each causality represents a story, a dream cut short, and a future denied.

Let *Will I Be Next? Gun Violence in America* be a call to action, an invitation to confront the uncomfortable truths about our society, and a roadmap toward a safer and more compassionate future. Together, we can challenge the status quo, dismantle the barriers that enable gun violence, and create a world where the haunting question of *Will I Be Next?* becomes a thing of the past.

Anthony F. Verdi, Ph.D.
Psychologist

Acknowledgments

As we express our gratitude, we must never forget that the highest appreciation is not to utter words but to live by them.

—John Fitzgerald Kennedy

I appreciate Robert W. Hollenbeck's devotion, love, insight, and copyediting of this book. To my friend and mentor, Father Benedict Reid, I extend my reverence for instilling in me that the perfect doctrine is the one you design for yourself and, more pointedly, that propels you to explore and fill that emptiness within you. I will forever miss you since you departed for *Shores Unknown.*

I am indebted to José Antonio Franceschini-Carlo, M.D., Professor and Chair of Psychiatry at Universidad Central del Caribe School of Medicine in Bayamón, Puerto Rico. His weekly radio program, *Déjame Ayudarte* (*Let Me Help You*), addresses the rampant gun violence, homophobia, misogyny, and predatory practices that pervade our society, driving many to suicide. I applaud his philosophy, which he expresses so well in one of his books, *Live Your Fullest Life.*

I am indebted to Dr. Anthony (Tony) Verdi for his kind introduction to this book. Tony has been a dynamic leader with over 40 years of experience working in hospitals and corporate settings. As a clinician and manager, Tony has helped individuals, groups, and organizations meet their goals. Furthermore, Tony has been a national healthcare management corporation executive for several years. A graduate of The University of Pennsylvania (B.A.) and Temple University (M.Ed., Ph.D.), Tony is a consultant and trainer to national corporations, non-profits, and small businesses. As a licensed psychologist, he maintains a private practice in psychology and coaching.

Tony has been practicing psychology since 1980 and joined the coaching community in 2006 to use his skills and life-long experiences to mentor the development of others. Tony recently moved from Philadelphia, Pennsylvania, to Palm Springs, California.

Dedication

The Gun Violence Archive reported that at least 4,994 people have died by guns in the US as of February 16, 2024.[1] Taken together, more than 13,900 people were killed in 2023 during these mass slaughters, an average of 115 deaths daily.[2]

Those mass murders, excluding the shooter, occurred nationwide, from Florida, Chicago to Mississippi, and Tennessee to Texas. Among those who died, 85 were children, and 491 were teenagers. The carnage happened in innumerable shopping centers, schools, parties, and neighborhoods. Outside of war and conflict zones, no industrialized nation besides the United States has experienced such a Herculean bloodbath in civic life.

After the massacre at Allen, the affluent suburb of Dallas, Texas, Representative Sheila Jackson Lee said:

---

[1]   www.gunviolencearchive.org, Feb 16, 2024

[2]   Alfonseca, K.: "More than 13,900 people killed in gun violence so far in 2023." *ABC News.* May 2, 2023. https://abcnews.go.com/US/116-people-died-gun-violence-day-us-year/story?id=97382759

"I'm just so tired and hurt and devastated by the continuing mass shootings in this state and this nation… Eight innocent people are dead— dead by gunfire. Guns again.

Of course, I offer my prayers and concerns for those families struggling with losing their loved ones. But I also ask: 'When will we confront the real cause?' And that is a proliferation of guns, guns, guns."

Senate Chaplain Barry C. Black, who rarely expresses personal views, indicated, as he delivered morning prayers:

"When babies die at a church school, it is time for us to move beyond thoughts and prayers."

This book is dedicated to those who lost their lives, especially innocent children and the elderly. It is also dedicated to the courageous first responders, those who risked their lives to save these souls, and the healthcare providers who tended to the wounded survivors.[3]

---

[3] For details of the recent mass shootings in the United States, the reader is referred to *Wikipedia, the free encyclopedia*: "List of mass shootings in the United States in 2024." March 2, 2024. https://en.wikipedia. org/wiki/List_of_mass_shootings_in_the_United_States_in_2024.

Prologue

"By right we arm but by love disarm."

—Agona Apell

The pervasive occurrence of gun violence in America poses a severe and constant danger to our fundamental entitlement: the right to life. Over 600 individuals perish daily due to the occurrence of firearm-related violence. This phenomenon is partially fueled by the convenient availability of firearms, regardless of their legality. Nothing will stop a man from taking the life of another, like codes that prevent him from acquiring the means to do so.

The gunning down of so many defenseless persons is defied by logic. When we hear of yet another senseless massacre against strangers in a public setting in the United States, especially in a school filled with innocent children, that is the logical question that comes to mind. In the past 50 years, shooting deaths of Americans outnumbered those lost in all the country's wars combined.

It saddens me that we live in a society where the love for guns is so intercalated into the genome of so many. It is so difficult for us to understand that guns have one purpose and only one purpose: to kill. What causes a society to be influenced by dogmata that promote repugnance against human beings... against anyone different? Why is it that so many of us are so pro-life yet disregard that the current cause of death in children and adolescents in the US is attributable to gun violence?[4]

Why is it so challenging to understand that arms limitations can save lives? Contrary to what many imply, Serious Mental Illness (SMI) has little to do with killing by firearms. To summarize Rozel and Swanson,[5] it's tempting to say gun violence is about mental illness, albeit the truth is much more complex... it distracts people from the real issue regarding guns and mental health. Not all mass murderers suffer from SMI, even though their motivation may be a mental condition. Even when compared to other developed countries, our rate of gun violence is far higher, according to statistics, even when the prevalence of mental illness is comparable. Indeed, a substantial eradication of mental disorders would only lead to a 4% drop in gun

4   Goldstick, J.E., Cunningham, R.M., and Carter, P.M.: Correspondence to the Editor, "Current Causes of Death in Children and Adolescents in the United States. N Eng J Med. 2022; 386: 1955-1956.

5   Rozel, J. and Swanson, J: "It's tempting to say gun violence is about mental illness." AMMC (Jan 26, 2023): https://www.aamc.org/news/it-s-tempting-say-gun-violence-about-mental-illness-truth-much-more-complex.

violence. Most violent crimes, including homicides, would still occur.

Suicide victims armed with firearms also have an even lower prevalence of mental disease diagnoses. According to the available research, there is only a modest correlation between mental illness and suicide ideation and actions.[6]

Science is clear.[7] Arms limitation saves lives. We must take firearms off our streets, as has been done in other countries. This is particularly important for the most dangerous guns in America.[8] These include pistols, revolvers, rifles, shotguns, and derringers. Simple legislation to make weapons safer and more challenging to purchase can put an end to killings like the ones in Uvalde and Buffalo. This is especially true for weapons of mass destruction with high-capacity magazines, including the AR-15-style semi-automatic weapon (called a DDM4-style rifle). These are firearms that gun-control advocates indicate aren't any different from the civilian versions of a military weapon.

The minimum age required to purchase weapons should be raised to 25. Mental health professionals

---

[6] *"Mental Illness and Gun Violence."* Johns Hopkins Center for Gun Violence Solutions, CDC Wonder Data Base (2017). https://efsgv.org/learn/learn-more-about-gun-violence/mental-illness-and-gun-violence/

[7] The Editors: "The Science is Clear: Gun Control Saves Lives." *Scientific American.* May 26, 2022. https://www.scientificamerican.com/article/the-science-is-clear-gun-control-saves-lives/.

[8] Rolling Stone: "The 5 Most Dangerous Guns in America. These Are the Firearms causing the most harm." Rolling Stone. July 14, 2014. https://www.rollingstone.com/culture/culture-lists/the-5-most-dangerous-guns-in-america-22699/pistols-253847/.

agree that an adolescent's brain is not fully developed until the age of 25 or so, making these young adults more likely to act impulsively.[9] Most adults process information with the left prefrontal cortex (the rational region of the brain). It is the region that responds with appropriate judgment in stressful situations. Adolescents respond with the amygdala, the emotional region of the brain. The connections between the emotional and the decision-making centers do not fully develop simultaneously in adolescents. That is why when young adults react emotionally and impulsively, they cannot explain their thoughts.

The media's coverage of mass shootings is another crucial factor to consider. Reports of violent incidents are often widely covered in the press and quickly shared on social media and other mass platforms. Professionals worry that people may be inspired to replicate these crimes after seeing them covered in the media.[10] This is commonly referred to as the *media contagion effect*, and it occurs in instances of suicide, terrorism, and mass carnage.

The senseless deaths of so many innocent people in our country each year due to gun violence are inexplicable. Again, restricting weapons from public areas is the simple solution, as other countries have

---

[9] Jensen, F., and Nutt, A. E.: p. 103. *The Teenage Brain: A Neuroscientist's Survival Guide to Raising Adolescents and Young Adults.* (New York: Harper), 2016.

[10] Thompson, D.: "Mass Shootings in America Are Spreading Like a Disease." *The Atlantic.* Retrieved March 14, 2018, fromhttps://www.theatlantic.com/health/archive/2017/11/americas-mass-shooting-epidemic-contagious/545078/.

done. Or, at a bare minimum, outlaw assault weapons (such as AR-15 rifles) and firearms with high-capacity magazines, increase the age for purchasing firearms to 25, regulate the promotion and sale of guns and ammunition, insist on background checks before selling a firearm, impose rigorous requirements for owning firearms, use biometric firearm authentication methods, end legal immunity for gun manufacturers, reduce firearm access to youth and individuals who are at risk of harming themselves or others, support gun violence research, demand that firearms owners receive training and licensing, vote against anti-gun control politicians, and insist on safe storage of weapons.

Are our leaders unwilling to reexamine the pros and cons of the National Rifle Association and the Second Amendment to the US Constitution to protect us and our human rights by not tackling and putting an end to this epidemic of gun violence and gun deaths?

Chapter 1

The National Rifle Association (NRA)

When it first came into being in 1871, the National Rifle Association's stated goal was to "promote and encourage rifle shooting on a scientific basis."

The only requirement for a National Rifle Association (NRA) membership is the willingness to give the organization $25 to $35 per year to be a member. That's it. There are no other requirements. Anyone person with an interest in firearms can become a member.[11] The benefits include:

- Personal firearms insurance
- Life, health, and accident insurance and travel assistance
- 24/7 defense of your gun rights

---

[11] www.benefits.nra.org

- Property and liability insurance
- Membership in the PenFed Credit Union
- Identity theft protection
- Emergency Assistance Plus
- Membership in a Wine Club
- Membership in the NRA Travel Center
- Membership in the NRA Cigar Club
- News and Entertainment
- Patriot Mobile
- NRA Outdoor Adventure and Hunting License Partner
- Cancer Care
- NRA Licensed Products

Plus, the NRA 5-Star Benefits, which put hundreds of dollars back in your pocket!

The Disarray of the NRA

The NRA is now among the most powerful political groups in the United States. Still, the NRA's disarray may be news to you.[12]

The organization "has illegally coordinated with multiple political campaigns—violating a federal law that prevents independent groups from synchronizing

---

[12] "The NRA Is in Disarray: Here's What You Need to Know." *Giffords Courage to Fight Gun Violence.* May 24, 2022. https://giffords.org/blog/2022/05/nra-in-disarray-what-you-need-to-know-blog/.

their efforts with campaigns. Four complaints filed at the Federal Election Commission (FEC) by the Campaign Legal Center (CLC) and Giffords accused the NRA of illegally coordinating with the campaigns of multiple GOP senate candidates in the 2014, 2016, and 2018 election cycles." In addition, "Giffords and CLC also filed FEC complaints documenting illegal campaign coordination involving the NRA and the Trump presidential campaign. The group spent $25 million, mostly on television ads, through the same companies—and often the same executives—who placed spots for the Trump campaign, violating well-established campaign finance laws." Also, "In the aftermath of the leadership struggle, the NRA filed a lawsuit in New York against North over the failed takeover and his secret fiduciary relationship with Ackerman McQueen, stating 'simply put, the NRA exists to fight for the Second Amendment—not pay other people's bills.'" Furthermore, "In November 2021, it was revealed in secret recordings obtained by NPR that leaders of the NRA struggled with how to respond after the Columbine shooting in 1999. On the tapes, officials are heard rejecting a fund for victims and settling on a destructive message that has shaped the organization's response to mass shootings in the decades since."

Astonishingly, after the suspicions of corruption appeared, the NRA lost over one million members, according to financial documents that were released in November 2022 and August 2021.[13] Much of the drop in membership is also attributed to the horrific tragedies that inspired the first significant trends to impose federal gun regulations in a generation.

But even if the NRA is in disarray, the organization spends tens of millions annually on political and legal activism and gun safety training. Additionally, it backs a network of state organizations operating around the country, such as the New York State Rifle and Pistol Association, which last year prevailed in a significant Supreme Court decision involving American gun rights. Nonetheless, the corruption charges have negatively impacted the group's capacity to draw new members and keep them engaged.

And if that weren't enough, a Manhattan jury found three top executives of the NRA liable in a lengthy civil trial that focused on alleged corruption and the misspending of millions of dollars. The jury concluded these executives "had caused roughly $5.4 million worth of harm to the nonprofit group's finances—though they also found that LaPierre had already repaid about $1 million."[14]

On the positive side, the NRA codes abolished child labor and established the precedent of federal

---

[13] Gutowski, S.: "The NRA has lost over a million members since corrupt allegations surfaced." *The Reload*. Feb. 9, 2023. https://thereload.com/nra-has-lost-over-a-million-members-since-corruption-allegations-surfaced/.

[14] Mann, B. and Bowman, M.: "Jury finds NRA, Wayne LaPierre liable in civil corruption case." NPR Newsletter. Feb.23, 2024. https://www.npr.org/2024/02/23/1232229060/nra-wayne-lapierre-corruption-trial-verdict-new-york.

regulation of minimum wages and maximum hours. The organization also helped the labor movement by establishing many low-skilled employee unions.[15] In other words, it encouraged the creation of industry-wide codes that set standards for fair competition, labor conditions, and pricing.

Nonetheless, the organization is laden with significant scrutiny following high-profile shootings that have claimed many innocent lives. Many are against the organization because it lobbies heavily against all forms of gun control and unfalteringly defends the Second Amendment of the Constitution, which questionably gives US citizens the right to bear arms.

---

[15] Digitalhistory.edu

Chapter 2

The Second Amendment to the US Constitution

The Second Amendment of the United States Constitution states, "A well-regulated Militia, being necessary to the security of a free State, the right of the people to keep and bear Arms, shall not be infringed."

The Central Question

Using such terminology has sparked significant controversy on the intended extent of the Amendment. Debates about the amendment have questioned whether the protection is for the right of a private citizen to keep a firearm for self-defense or whether security is to be exercised through a militia, such as the

National Guard or the Armed Forces. This means that the amendment is plagued with pros and cons.[16]

This argument was not voiced by politicians, much less by the public, until decades after the Bill of Rights was enacted. Nevertheless, the stated objective of the discussion has been to lessen the tragic loss of life caused by armed murder. Thus, many firearms and Constitution experts believe that the focus on the Second Amendment is frequently misplaced.

In an *Art of the Rifle* article, Jeff Cooper wrote shortly after the Second Amendment was enacted.

> *"The rifle itself has no moral stature since it has no will. Naturally, it may be used by evil men for evil purposes, but there are more good men than evil. While the latter cannot be persuaded to the path of righteousness by propaganda, they can certainly be corrected by good men with rifles."*

The Pros of the Amendment

- The possession of firearms reduces many types of crime in society.
- The amendment allows individuals to defend themselves.

---

[16] Regoli, N., Editor in Chief: "17 Big Pros and Cons of the 2nd Amendment." *Connect Us.* Apr. 20, 2019. https://connectusfund. org/8-big-pros-and-cons-of-the-2nd-amendment

- The amendment strengthens the Constitution's laws under its inclusion in the Bill of Rights.
- The amendment enables the average citizen to defend the nation.
- The amendment permits a well-regulated militia to be an integral element of American culture.
- To possess a firearm in the United States, an individual must qualify.
- The amendment provides society with additional checks and balances.

The Cons of the Amendment

On the other hand, problems exist with the Second Amendment.

- The amendment does not provide for the secure application and use of firearms in society.
- The amendment does not define what counts as a firearm.
- There is no guarantee that a firearms expert will be present during a violent firearm attack.
- Possession of a firearm increases the likelihood of harm to the owner and the owner's household.
- There are multiple alternatives to firearms ownership for deterring crime.
- Possession of a firearm increases the likelihood of domestic violence.

- It is well established that the current gun-control laws are ineffective.

- Laws that allow the carrying of firearms openly increase costs associated with law enforcement.

- For many, the amendment interpretation has fallen into desuetude. Implying that the more recent interpretation of the amendment has shifted from its original meaning.

- The amendment does not mention the cost of ownership as a component of an individual's rights as an American.

- The amendment does not exclude specific actions, behaviors, choices, or states of mind.

We must also remember that when our Forefathers drafted the Second Amendment, the prevalent weaponry was muskets and flintlock pistols. Each firearm had a capacity of one round, and a proficient shooter could potentially discharge three or even four shots within a minute of shooting. According to all reports, they were not particularly precise either. Nowadays, gunmen looking to harm as many individuals as possible in the shortest time imaginable favor assault rifles like the AR-15, with a magazine capacity of 30 rounds, capable of firing 45 rounds per minute, with a muzzle velocity of 3,260 feet per second, and a maximum accurate range of 550 meters.[17]

---

[17]　Ingraham C.: "What 'arms' looked like when the Second Amendment was written." *Washington Post.* Jun. 13, 2016. https://www.washing-

To conclude, it's essential to note that many, especially congressmen and senators, read and interpret the main pros and cons of the Second Amendment as an echo chamber about issues concerning gun control instead of engaging in conversations with others.

As some have said, as the image below depicts, "A Well-regulated Militia Doesn't Kill Children."[18]

tonpost.com/news/wonk/wp/2016/06/13/the-men-who-wrote-the-2nd-amendment-would-never-recognize-an-ar-15/.

[18] Photograph from: "Student riot at the Capitol for gun control." Iowa Public Radio, BBC Service, Apr. 20, 2018. https://www.iowapublicradio.org/ipr-news/2018-04-20/students-rally-at-the-capitol-for-gun-control

Chapter 3

The Courts and Legislation

Leading gun-rights proponents quickly realized that the Supreme Court's Bruen decision on the Second Amendment would fundamentally alter the legal battle over who has access to weapons.[19, 20] The Supreme Court of the United States (SCOTUS) justices are ideologically divided, with six conservatives against and three liberals for arms limitation. The laws intended to offer some leeway in deciding whether to grant a license to gun owners. In resumé, the Supreme Court

---

[19] Sneed, T.: "How the Supreme Court put gun control laws in jeopardy nationwide." *CNN Politics.* October 10, 2022, https://www.cnn.com/2022/10/09/politics/gun-control-second-amendment-supreme-court-bruen-fallout/index.html.

[20] Gresko, J.: "Supreme Court strikes down New York law restricting guns outside the home, with implications for other states." *PBS News Hour.* June 23, 2022. https://www.pbs.org/newshour/politics/in-major-ruling-for-gun-rights-supreme-court-strikes-down-new-york-law-on-firearm-permits.

significantly curtailed a state's ability to restrict citizens' right to carry firearms publicly for self-defense.

Notwithstanding, as more politicians lose loved ones due to mass shootings, they begin to see how the government is turning a blind eye to gun control measures. As a result, many legislators are hoping to see more gun control against the carnage that's taking place in our country.[21] Furthermore, those in positions of power are sponsoring measures to, for example, ban the possession of high-capacity magazines.

Recently, California attempted to implement a law to restrict the sale and use of handguns, but almost immediately, a federal judge blocked key provisions of that law.[22] In a ruling, Judge Cormac Carney argued that "requirements for new handguns are unconstitutional and cannot be enforced."

But in a statement, Attorney General Rob Bonta said, "The fact of the matter is, California's gun safety laws save lives, and California's Unsafe Handgun Act is no exception. We will continue to lead efforts to advance and defend California's gun safety laws. As we determine the next steps in this case, Californians should know that this injunction has not gone into effect and that California's important gun safety

[21] Aning, A.K.: "As More Politicians Lose Friends and Family to Gun Violence, Will It Change How They Govern?" *The Trace.* April 18, 2023, https://www.thetrace.org/2023/04/mass-shootings-politicians-gun-reform/.

[22] Dazio, S.: "Federal judge blocks key parts of California handgun law. *AP News.* March 20, 2022. https://apnews.com/article/california-gun-control-supreme-court-1b5bbef296f16c8f56fd16f75555c044.

requirements related to the Unsafe Handgun Act remain in effect."

It is important to note that California has the strictest gun laws and that the state has the seventh lowest death rate due to gun violence in our country. The state's gun regulations include funding for community initiatives that have decreased gun-related violence and controlling who can buy a gun and what kinds of firearms are legally attainable.[23]

This is followed by Illinois, Connecticut, New Jersey, New York, Hawaii, Maryland, and Massachusetts. Many of these states require background checks and waiting periods before anyone is allowed to purchase a gun. Some require that individuals undergo training before buying a firearm.

So, it appears that progress against the massacres might be forthcoming.

---

[23] "Strictest Gun Laws by State" *World Population Review*. Updated April 2023. https://worldpopulationreview.com/state-rankings/ strictest-gun-laws-by-state.

Chapter 4

Anger and Guns

The American Psychological Association defines anger as "an emotion characterized by tension and hostility arising from frustration, real or imagined injury by another, or perceived injustice. It can manifest in behaviors designed to remove the object of the anger (e.g., determined action) or behaviors designed merely to express the emotion (e.g., swearing). Anger is distinct from, but a significant activator of, aggression, which is behavior intended to harm someone or something. Despite their mutually influential relationship, anger is neither necessary nor sufficient for aggression to occur."[24]

The National Comorbidity Study Replication has conducted analyses that offer the initial nationally representative estimates of the simultaneous presence

---

[24] APA Dictionary of Psychology: https://dictionary.apa.org/.

of pathological anger traits and the possession or carrying of a firearm among individuals, considering specific mental illnesses and demographic variables.[25] The findings of this study indicate that a significant number of individuals in the United States exhibit anger features and also own firearms at their residence (10.4%) or carry guns outside their residence (1.6%). This dataset provides evidence of the correlations between many prevalent mental diseases and different anger tendencies in relation to access to firearms. Due to the low rate of hospitalization for mental health issues among individuals with this specific combination, most of them will not be affected by current legal limitations on firearm possession connected to involuntary commitment. It is unlikely to be practical to exclude a significant section of the general population from possessing guns. Implementing behavioral risk-based strategies for weapons restriction, such as broadening the criteria for individuals forbidden from owning guns to encompass those with violent misdemeanor convictions and numerous DUI convictions, may serve as a more efficacious public health measure in curbing gun violence within the population.

Notwithstanding its negative aspects, anger can foster a sense of optimism and motivate us to concentrate on our desired achievements. It can enhance one's chances of survival and instill a feeling of dominance instead

---

[25] Swanson, J.W., Sampson, N.A., Petukhova, M.V., et al: "Guns, Impulsive Angry Behavior, and Mental Disorders: Results from the National Comorbidity Survey Replication (NCS-R), Behavioral Science and the Law, 8 Apr. 2015. https://doi.org/10.1002/bsl.2172.

of fixating on pain, mistreatment, or victimization. It's an emotion that can motivate us to solve problems and make us aware of injustices and goals we want to achieve. It can enable us to constructively comprehend, utilize, and regulate our emotions to alleviate stress, communicate proficiently, demonstrate empathy towards others, surmount obstacles, and resolve conflicts.

Yet, as stated above, contrary to what many imply, mental illness has little to do with killing by firearms. My premise continues to be that nothing will keep human beings from committing homicide than decrees that prevent them from acquiring the means to do so.

Whether legal or illegal, armed violence continues to threaten our fundamental right to life. As already stated, more than 600 human beings succumbed because of shootings in the US. Although anyone can be affected, people of color, women, children, those in deprived communities, and other marginalized groups are most often disproportionately affected.

The simple presence of a firearm can make an individual feel threatened or afraid to go out of their homes. Such fear can interrupt access to education and healthcare and daily living activities such as shopping or attending sports events.

Another thing we must consider is that most deaths caused by firearms occur outside of armed conflict settings such as wars and that in many states, more than half of deaths caused by guns are due to suicides or accidents.

In conclusion, the presence of pathological anger coupled with the possession of a firearm continues to present a serious problem in our society. So, again, I emphasize that the way to keep human beings from killing each other is to restrict the means that allow them to do so.

Chapter 5

Gun-Related Deaths in Countries Other than the US

It's beyond the scope of this book to consider gun control in all countries outside the US. Nevertheless, the following are highlighted.

Puerto Rico

Puerto Rico, nicknamed La Isla del Encanto (Island of Enchantment), is included here because many Puerto Ricans consider the country independent, even though it has not become a State of the Union. The Commonwealth of Puerto Rico is a self-governing Caribbean Island and an unincorporated territory of the US.

When compared to the other 50 states and the District of Columbia, Puerto Rico has a much higher rate of gun violence. This information is derived from the Puerto Rico Violent Death Reporting System, which is a component of a nationwide system that documents all types of violent fatalities in the District of Columbia, the fifty states, and Puerto Rico.[26] In the United States, Puerto Rico has one of the most alarmingly high rates of gun violence. Puerto Rico's total gun death rate would rank seventh among the 50 states. Approximately 660 individuals lose their lives each year due to gun violence in the area, with over 93% of these casualties being homicides.

Canada

On May 1, 2020, more than 1,500 firearm models were added to the list of prohibited, restricted, or non-restricted items in the Criminal Code's Regulations Prescribing Certain Firearms and Other Weapons, Components, and Parts of Weapons, Accessories, Cartridge Magazines, Ammunition, and Projectiles. Some parts of recently outlawed weapons, such as the upper receivers of AR-15, M4, M16, and AR-10 models, are also included in the ban. Sniper rifles and other weapons with muzzle energies exceeding 10,000 Joules and barrel diameters of 20 mm or larger are now considered to have satisfied the new maximum

---

[26] Nguyen, A.: "A Year Later: Gun Violence in the US Territories." *GIFFORDS*. Apr. 17, 2023. https://giffords.org/blog/2023/04/a-year-later-gun-violence-in-the-us-territories/

standards. Owning any firearm that is longer or heavier than these is currently illegal.[27]

Australia

According to the latest Australian government data on crime trends, homicide rates have been decreasing for the past quarter of a century. As of right now, the murder rate is at its lowest point in the last quarter of a century.[28]

Israel

The National Security Ministry recently released statistics showing that only approximately 2.6% of Israeli adults, or 150,000 people, have a personal gun license. Not included in this total are the weapons possessed by security personnel (such as IDF soldiers, police, and border guards), as well as the estimated 400,000 illicit firearms, the great majority of which are circulated among Arab neighborhoods.[29]

---

[27] "Changes to Prohibited Firearms." *Public Safety Canada*. Feb. 3, 2023. https://www.publicsafety.gc.ca/cnt/cntrng-crm/frrms/pafqa-afaqa-en.aspx.

[28] Kiley, E.: "Gun Control in Australia, Updated." Factcheck.org. Oct. 6, 2017. https://www.publicsafety.gc.ca/cnt/cntrng-crm/frrms/pafqa-afaqa-en.aspx.

[29] Koningsveld, A.V.: "Firearm Licensing in Israel: How Strict Are the Jewish State's Gun Laws?" *The Algemeiner*. Feb. 27, 2023. https://www.algemeiner.com/2023/02/27/firearm-licensing-in-israel-how-strict-are-the-jewish-states-gun-laws/.

The United Kingdom

The public's ability to acquire weapons in the UK is governed by some of the most stringent regulations globally. Public members can own rifles and shotguns with a valid license. The 1996 Dunblane school tragedy, however, led to the banning of most firearms in the United Kingdom. In accordance with their laws, Northern Ireland, the Channel Islands, and the Isle of Man all permit the carrying of handguns. Unlike England and Wales, Scotland has its own licensing system for air guns.[30]

Norway

Norway has rigorous regulations for gun licenses, even though the country has over 1.2 million registered firearms. A gun license can be obtained for hunting or sporting purposes, but not for target practice. One must be at least 18 to purchase a hunting rifle, and at least 21 to purchase a handgun. To obtain a hunting license, you must take a 30-hour course and pass an exam on the responsible handling of the firearm and how hunting affects ecosystems. After passing the exam, if you wish to hunt with a firearm, you must register with the government and get a license. A completed application must be submitted to a police station to acquire a firearm. The applicant must indicate the intended purpose of the firearm as part

---

[30] Wikipedia: "Firearms regulations in the United Kingdom. https://en.wikipedia.org/wiki/Firearms_regulation_in_the_United_Kingdom.

of the application. For hunters, the rule is eight guns, with a limit of one weapon per caliber. Hunting permits must be renewed each year.[31]

Japan

The assassination of former Japanese prime minister Shinzo Abe was startling, given that Japan has some of the strictest gun control laws in the world and comparatively few gun-related deaths compared to the US. For example, in 2018, there were nine firearms deaths in Japan, which is incredibly low compared to the 39,740 in the US, where 13,958 people were killed by gun violence, according to a 2020 report from the Johns Hopkins Center for Gun Violence Solutions.[32]

China

In China, protecting state-owned property (such as the arms industry, financial institutions, resource storage, and scientific research facilities) allows the legitimate use of firearms. This includes law enforcement, the military, paramilitary groups, and security professionals. The main reason why people

[31] Norwell, F: "EXPLAINED: What are Norway's gun control laws?" *The Local no.* Jun. 27, 2022. https://www.thelocal.no/20220627/explained-what-are-norways-gun-control-laws.

[32] Bushard, B: "Here's How Japan's Low Gun Death Rate Compares To the U.S. And Other Countries." *FORBES.* Jul. 8. https://www.forbes.com/sites/brianbushard/2022/07/08/heres-how-japans-low-gun-death-rate-compares-to-the-us-and-other-countries/?sh=25f8429758c42022.

can still own guns is for hunting, which is an exception to the overall ban. Those possessing valid hunting licenses are authorized to apply for and possess firearms intended for hunting. There is a death penalty for gun crimes and a minimum sentence of three years in jail for illegal gun ownership or sale.[33]

Philippines

Strong societal standards act as a brake on random acts of violence. A criminology associate professor at Southern Illinois University and a former inmate named Raymund Narag claim that the Tagalog word hiyâ, meaning shame or humiliation, plays a role in preventing mass shootings in the Philippines. It is commonly said that a fundamental value in the Philippines is to avoid hiyâ and to protect one's family and community from it. "It reflects on you and your family," Narag says. "When I was jailed, our entire clan felt humiliated."[34]

---

[33]   Wikipedia: "Gun control in China." https://en.wikipedia.org/wiki/Gun_control_in_China.

[34]   De Guzman, C: "One Surprising Theory Why the Philippines Has Very Few Mass Shootings—Despite Easy Access To Lots of Guns." *TIME*. Jun. 15, 2022. https://time.com/6186982/philippines-guns-mass-shootings/.

Singapore

According to several recent measurements and calculations spanning many years, the global rate of firearm-related deaths is lowest in Singapore.[35]

Taiwan

Taiwan approved new provisions to an existing law that criminalizes the open display of firearms (including replicas) and imposes severe punishments on those found guilty. Under the revised Controlling Guns, Ammunition, and Knives Act, anyone found guilty of public or easily accessible discharge of a standard firearm in a public area might be fined up to $479 and sentenced to at least seven years in prison. Seizures of newly modified firearms implicated in instances resulting in casualties prompted the Ministry of the Interior (MOI) to propose the change. Before the amendment's passage, firearm discharge in public was not considered a crime under Taiwan's Criminal Code.[36]

---

[35] Wikipedia: "List of countries by firearms-related death rate." https://en.wikipedia.org/wiki/List_of_countries_by_firearm-related_death_rate.

[36] Editor: "Taiwan passes law to curb use of firearms in public." *FOCUS TAIWAN*. Dec. 10, 2023. https://focustaiwan.tw/politics/202312180014.

Switzerland

Based on statistics from the Global Health Data Exchange, the gun homicide rate in Switzerland in 2019 was approximately 0.2 per 100,000 residents. This number is comparable to other European countries and is 20 times lower than the rate observed in the United States. The world average is about three homicides per 100,000 people. In 2022, firearms were responsible for 11 homicides and nine attempted homicides in Switzerland.[37]

To reiterate, it is beyond the scope of this book to cover arms-related deaths in every country other than the US. The purpose of this chapter was to show that when we look at high-income countries and territories, the US is an exception when it comes to firearm homicides.[38]

---

[37] Guilléron, L.: © 2023 Keystone. "How Switzerland combines a passion for guns and safety." SWIswissinfo.ch. Dec. 2023. https://www.swissinfo.ch/eng/business/how-switzerland-combines-a-passion-for-guns-with-safety/49115108#:~:text=The%20specialists%20who%20spoke%20to,early%20age%2C%20and%20individual%20responsibility.

[38] Leach-Kemon, K., Sirull, R., and Glenn, S.: "On gun violence, the United States is an outlier." *INSTITUTE FOR HEALTH AND EVALUATION.* Oct. 31, 2023. https://www.healthdata.org/news-events/insights-blog/acting-data/gun-violence-united-states-outlier.

Chapter 6

Fear of Gun Violence

A recent survey on stress and mass shootings by the American Psychological Association (APA) indicates that mass shootings worry most US adults.[39] Likewise, many US adults say that the concern over mass shootings prevents them from attending places such as shopping malls, schools, movie theaters, grocery stores, or sporting events. This is particularly true for Hispanic and Black Americans, more so than for white non-Hispanics. And more women than men report feeling anxious about the possibility of being shot during a mass shooting. Numerous individuals believe they cannot go anywhere without fear of being the target of gun violence.

---

[39] Bethune, S. and Lewan, E: "One-Third of US Adults Say Fear of Mass Shootings Prevents Them from Going to Certain Places or Events." APA. Aug. 15, 2019. https://www.apa.org/news/press/releases/2019/08/fear-mass-shooting.

According to Dr. Arthur Evans, the chief executive officer of the APA, "It's clear that mass shootings are taking a toll on our mental health, and we should be particularly concerned that they are affecting the way many of us live our daily lives. The more these events happen in places where people can see themselves frequenting, the greater the mental health impact will be. We don't have to experience these events directly for them to affect us. Simply hearing about them can have an emotional impact, and this can have negative repercussions for our mental and physical health."[40]

The same thing can be said for several of the author's relatives from Europe, South America, and the Caribbean, who have indicated that they would not travel to the US to visit for fear of being gunned down.

Gun violence in the schools

Many parents worry that a radical mass shooter may enter a school and claim their child's life. Per the latest PBS NewsHour/NPR/Marist poll, in many neighborhoods, four out of ten Americans believe schools are prone to gun violence.[41] The number of communities affected by shootings and the feelings of worry are expanding. These concerns are primarily

---

[40] Ibid.

[41] Santhanam, L.: "Concern about gun violence in the schools is on the rise, new poll shows." *PBS Newshour*. May 25, 2023. https://www.pbs.org/newshour/politics/a-year-after-uvalde-support-rises-for-controlling-gun-violence.

due to the massacres that have increased by 10% since February 2019. This was one year after 19-year-old Nikolas Cruz opened fire at the school in Parkland, Florida, claiming 17 lives. Incidentally, Florida is a state where gun laws continue to be much less restrictive.

Even though six in ten Americans agree that controlling fire-arm-related violence is more important than protecting gun rights, we still must contend with the four in ten who think otherwise. When we think of the horrific mass murder at Uvalde, Texas, where 21 lives were lost, Reverend Evan McClanahan asked, "…what exact law should have been passed to prevent [such massacres]"?

Other Incidents Worth Mentioning

It has been well established that gun violence is the current leading cause of death in children and adolescents in the US. This is true, particularly in schools. Yet, mention must be made of other instances where arbitrary and abusive use of firearms has led to the loss of life.

For instance, recent, high-profile killings by gunfire when someone rang the wrong doorbell, pulled into the wrong driveway, or got into the wrong car. Why is it so ingrained into the genome of so many Americans to "stand your ground" and kill someone if they feel threatened or if their property has been invaded?

The American people are hardwired from birth to carry weapons. Many US citizens believe it is a divinely bestowed right, as stated in the Constitution, that citizens have the right to keep and bear arms. However, while guns have always been associated with security in recent years, public perception of the use of firearms has shifted. While most Americans either own guns or know someone who does, recent events have prompted calls to review the background check procedure for civilian weapon purchases.

What happened to the spirit of *ubuntu*? The fundamental meaning of *ubuntu*, an African proverb, is that everything we learn and experience in the world is through our relationships with others and that we are all one.[42]

So, for heaven's sake, let's be kind to one another. Let's stop gun violence.[43] Here is the evidence to support the idea that small actions can significantly impact. "When you know something works, you're going to lean in and help expand that," Nicole Hockley, co-founder and CEO of Sandy Hook Promise Foundation, says. "Our key message is that gun violence is preventable, and we have actions that every individual can take in their family, community, schools, and with politicians. Don't back away. Be part of the solution."

---

[42] Ibib. Goldstick, J.E., Cunningham, R.M., and Carter, P.M.

[43] Photograph from *The Sandy Hook Promise:* "What You Can Do Right Now to End Gun Violence." © Sandy Hook Promise 2024 Registered 501(c)(3). EIN: 46-1657101. https://www.sandyhookpromise.org/blog/student-resources/what-you-can-do-right-now-to-help-end-gun-violence/.

Conclusion

During the last five decades, deaths among Americans due to gun violence have outnumbered all lives lost in the country's wars combined.

If readers try to define the purpose of a gun, they will quickly discover that they cannot do so without using terms like "suitable for" or "intended for" or some other expression related to the use for which someone intends it.

Now, think of a gun. Most dictionary's broad definition is "a device that throws a projectile." Some may say it's "a device to use as a weapon to ensure self-defense, to protect others from criminals, or even to safeguard their property." That is what the Second Amendment of our Constitution grants us.

Others would say that a gun is "a device that throws projectiles that some, such as terrorists or hired killers, may use to kill others."

I say that a gun has one purpose and one purpose only: to kill, be it another human being or any living being.

Again, I ask the reader, why is mankind so influenced by belief systems that promote disgust against others… against anyone different? Why is there such a high level of xenophobia, misogyny, misopedia (hatred of children), and homophobia in our society? Therefore, the passion for guns is woven into the DNA of so many of us, and why is it so difficult to understand that gun policies can save lives? Even when we consider that the Second Amendment of our Constitution allows us to possess firearms, putatively, to defend ourselves, our property, and our country, why is this so challenging?

Does the amendment mean defending ourselves directly or through a "well-regulated militia," such as the National Guard? Have we stopped recognizing that when the amendment was drafted, the weapons available to the average American were muskets or flintlock pistols? Nowadays, those who attempt to massacre multitudes avail themselves of weapons of mass destruction and projectiles that can eviscerate the flesh or blow apart a skull in seconds, even at the risk of losing their own lives.

We live in a country that allegedly grants us inalienable rights: the rights to life, liberty, and the pursuit of happiness. In his article, Fairchild states, "Gun rights and freedom from gun violence are rights in our democracy. That is correct on moral, constitutional, and legal grounds."[44] Fairchild continues indicating that in a 2008 decision written for the majority by

---

[44]   Fairchild, P.: "Peter Fairchild: Think gun rights are inalienable? Read 'Heller.'" *Concord Monitor.* Jan. 7. 2019. https://www.concordmonitor. com/Gun-rights-and-gun-safety-22563890.

the late Justice Antonin Scalia, SCOTUS clarified and defined Second Amendment rights guaranteed by the Constitution for all citizens. Scalia confirmed that private gun ownership is a fundamental right, but "like most rights, the right safeguarded by the Second Amendment is *not infinite.*" [Italics mine.] To summarize, the amendment also protects restrictions on gun ownership, types, sales, carrying locations, and other issues related to public safety.[45]

Remember that the Constitution is a living, *amendable* document. However, changing the Constitution is challenging, and the Second Amendment could be repealed or modified. The only amendment that has ever been abolished with the introduction of the 21st Amendment is the 18th Amendment, which forbade the manufacture, transportation, and sale of alcohol.

One way would be for the proposed repeal or modification of the Second Amendment to be approved by the House and Senate with a two-thirds majority vote. Then, three-fourths of the states would need to approve the proposed repeal or amendment. The second method for repealing the Second Amendment would be a Constitutional Convention.

Once again, implementing gun restrictions in public settings is a straightforward and effective approach, as it has been successfully done in other countries. Alternatively, it is imperative to prohibit the possession of pistols, revolvers, rifles, shotguns, derringers, and firearms equipped with high-capacity magazines. Additionally, raising the minimum age for purchasing

---

[45]   Ibid. Fairchild, P.

firearms to 25, regulating the advertising and sale of guns and ammunition, mandating background checks before firearm transactions, implementing stringent requirements for firearm ownership, employing biometric firearm authentication methods, eliminating legal immunity for gun manufacturers, restricting firearm access for young individuals and those prone to self-harm or violence towards others, advocating for research on gun violence, enforcing mandatory training and licensing for firearm owners, opposing politicians who are against gun control measures, and enforcing secure storage of weapons are all necessary measures.

And we must ask ourselves, do our politicians refuse to reassess the advantages and disadvantages of the National Rifle Association and the Second Amendment to the US Constitution to safeguard our human rights by not addressing and resolving the widespread occurrence of gun violence and fatalities?

So, in the spirit of *ubuntu,* I end with, let's be kind to each other and not succumb to the massacres, carnage, fear, and anxiety created by the ongoing firearms-related violence in America. Let's not be the next victim. Let's live in a conventional, civilized society.

About the Author

Jaime R. Carlo-Casellas, Ph.D., September 15, 1943 –

My books address the notion that human suffering will always exist if superiority persists. We must recognize that we are selfless. Our human experience is meaningless or unworthy of analysis until we mindfully recognize what it means to be grateful for our well-being, to be happy, or until we question why we habitually inflict unhappiness on each other, where the seedbed of loathing, opprobrium, and odium resides.

As you will find in my books, it is now well-known that mindfulness can help you reap a cauldron of benefits, not to mention reach higher brain functioning, achieve loving-kindness toward others, and help manage emotional trauma, abuse, and addictive behavior.

My background includes a Ph.D. in Experimental Immunopathology, service as a Medical Service Corps Officer in the United States Navy during the Vietnam War, and Founding Director of the Stress

Management & Prevention Center, LLC, in Cathedral City, California.

To reach Jaime Carlo-Casellas:
email: casellas@stressprevention.org